The Story of
Little Black Sambo

Frontispiece

The Story of Little Black Sambo

BY
HELEN BANNERMAN

With Twenty-seven Illustrations

APPLEWOOD BOOKS
BEDFORD, MASSACHUSETTS

This edition of *Little Black Sambo* was originally published in 1921.

ISBN 1-55709-414-4

Thank you for purchasing an Applewood Book.
Applewood reprints America's lively classics — books
from the past that are of interest to modern readers.
For a free copy of our current catalog, write to:
Applewood Books, P.O. Box 365, Bedford, MA 01730.

10

Library of Congress Cataloging-in-Publication Data: 95-82095.

Printed in Singapore.

PREFACE

APPLEWOOD BOOKS is proud to re-issue this classic edition of *Little Black Sambo*. During the last thirty years, the book and its little hero have been the center of a big controversy. Sambo became, to some, a symbol of racism, and to others, he remained a long-remembered favorite.

Many may wonder why we are reissuing this book. As with all the books we publish, we are reissuing this book as a window on our past.

Recently, I read this book to my two young sons. When I asked them what they thought, they said they thought Sambo was a hero and marveled at his bravery.

—THE PUBLISHER

The Story of

Little Black Sambo

ONCE upon a time there was a little black boy, and his name was Little Black Sambo.

And his Mother was
called Black Mumbo.

And his Father was
called Black Jumbo.

And Black Mumbo
made him a beautiful
little Red Coat, and a

pair   of   beautiful   little
Blue Trousers.

15

And Black Jumbo went to the Bazaar, and bought him a beautiful Green Umbrella, and a lovely little Pair of Purple Shoes with Crimson Soles and Crimson Linings.

And then wasn't Little
Black Sambo
grand?

So he put on all his Fine Clothes, and went out for a walk in the Jungle. And by and by he met a Tiger. And the Tiger said to him, "Little Black Sambo, I'm going to eat you up!" And Little Black Sambo said, "Oh! Please, Mr. Tiger, don't eat me up, and I'll give you my

beautiful little Red Coat."
So the Tiger said, "Very
well, I won't eat you this
time, but you must give
me your beautiful little
Red Coat." So the Tiger
got poor Little Black
Sambo's beautiful little
Red Coat, and went away
saying, "Now I'm the
grandest Tiger in the
Jungle."

And Little Black Sambo went on, and by and by he met another Tiger, and it said to him, "Little Black Sambo, I'm going to eat you up!" And Little Black Sambo said, "Oh! Please, Mr. Tiger, don't eat me up, and I'll give you my beau-

25

tiful little Blue Trousers."
So the Tiger said, "Very
well, I won't eat you this
time, but you must give
me your beautiful little
Blue Trousers." So the
Tiger got poor Little
Black Sambo's beautiful
little Blue Trousers, and
went away saying, "Now
I'm the grandest Tiger
in the Jungle."

And Little Black Sambo went on, and by and by he met another tiger, and it said to him, "Little Black Sambo, I'm going to eat you up!" And Little Black Sambo said, "Oh! Please, Mr. Tiger, don't eat me up, and I'll give you my beautiful little Purple Shoes with

Crimson Soles and Crimson Linings."

But the Tiger said, "What use would your shoes be to me? I've got four feet, and you've got only two: you haven't got enough shoes for me."

But Little Black Sambo said, "You could wear them on your ears."

"So I could," said the Tiger: "that's a very good idea. Give them to me, and I won't eat you this time."

So the Tiger got poor Little Black Sambo's beautiful little Purple Shoes with Crimson Soles and Crimson Linings, and went away saying, "Now I'm the grandest Tiger in the Jungle."

And by and by Little Black Sambo met another Tiger, and it said to him,

"Little Black Sambo, I'm going to eat you up!" And Little Black Sambo said, "Oh! Please, Mr. Tiger, don't eat me up, and I'll give you my beautiful Green Umbrella." But the Tiger said, "How can I carry an umbrella, when I need all my paws for walking with?"

"You could tie a knot on your tail, and carry it that way," said Little Black Sambo. "So I could," said the Tiger. "Give it to me, and I won't eat you this time." So he got poor Little Black Sambo's beautiful Green Umbrella, and went away saying, "Now I'm the grandest Tiger in the Jungle."

And poor Little Black Sambo went away crying, because the cruel Tigers had taken all his fine clothes.

Presently he heard a horrible noise that sounded like "Gr-r-r-r-r-rrrrrrr," and it got louder and louder. "Oh! dear!" said Little Black Sambo, "there are all the Tigers coming back to eat me up! What shall I do?" So he ran quickly to a palm-tree, and peeped round it to see what the matter was.

And there he saw all the Tigers fighting, and disputing which of them was the grandest. And at last they all got so angry that they jumped up and took off all the fine clothes, and began to tear each other with their claws, and bite each other with their great big white teeth.

And they came, rolling and tumbling, right to the foot of the very tree where Little Black Sambo was hiding, but he jumped quickly in behind the umbrella. And the Tigers all caught hold of each others' tails, as they wrangled and scrambled, and so they found themselves in a ring round the tree.

Then, while the Tigers were wrangling and scrambling, Little Black Sambo jumped up, and called out, "Oh! Tigers! Why have you taken off all your nice clothes? Don't you want them any more?" But the Tigers only answered, "Gr-r-rrrr!"

Then Little Black Sam-
bo said, "If you want them,
say so, or I'll take them
away." But the Tigers
would not let go of each
others' tails, and so they
could only say, "Gr-r-
r-r-rrrrrrr!"

So Little Black Sambo
put on all his fine clothes
again and walked off.

And the Tigers were
very, very angry, but still
they would not let go of
each others' tails.   And
they were so angry that
they ran round the tree,
trying to eat each other
up, and they ran faster
and faster, till they were
whirling round so fast
that you couldn't see
their legs at all.

And they still ran faster and faster and faster, till they all just melted away, and there was nothing left but a great big pool of melted butter (or "ghi," as it is called in India) round the foot of the tree.

Now Black Jumbo was just coming home from his work, with a great big brass pot in his arms, and when he saw what was left of all the Tigers he said, "Oh! what lovely melted butter! I'll take that home to Black Mumbo for her to cook with."

So he put it all into the great big brass pot, and took it home to Black Mumbo to cook with.

When Black Mumbo saw the melted butter, wasn't she pleased! "Now," said she, "we'll all have pancakes for supper!"

So she got flour and eggs and milk and sugar and butter, and she made a huge big plate of most lovely pancakes. And she fried them in the melted butter which the Tigers had made, and they were just as yellow and brown as little Tigers.

And then they all sat down to supper. And Black Mumbo ate Twenty-seven pancakes, and Black Jumbo ate Fifty-five, but Little Black Sambo ate a Hundred and Sixty-nine, because he was so hungry.

61

THE
END